Solos for Young Violists

Compiled and Edited by Violist **Barbara Barber**

Viola by Christian Pederson, Albuquerque, 2002
From the collection of Robertson & Sons Violin Shop Inc., Albuquerque, NM
Photo by Justin Robertson

Art Design: Ernesto Ebanks

© 2004 Summy-Birchard Music
a division of Summy-Birchard Inc.
All Rights Reserved   Printed in USA

ISBN 1-58951-188-3

Summy-Birchard Inc.
exclusively distributed by
Alfred Publishing Co., Inc.

INTRODUCTION

Solos for Young Violists is a five-volume series of music books with companion CDs featuring 34 works for viola and piano. Many of the pieces in this collection have long been recognized as stepping stones to the major viola repertoire, while others are newly discovered, arranged and published for this series; most are premier recordings. Compiled, edited and recorded by violist Barbara Barber, *Solos for Young Violists* is a graded series of works ranging from elementary to advanced levels and represents an exciting variety of styles and techniques for violists. The collection has become a valuable resource for teachers and students of all ages. The piano track recorded on the second half of each CD gives the violist the opportunity to practice with accompaniments.

Contents

Passacaglia
on an Old English Tune*

Rebecca Clarke
1886-1979

Grave, ma non troppo lento ♩ = 66

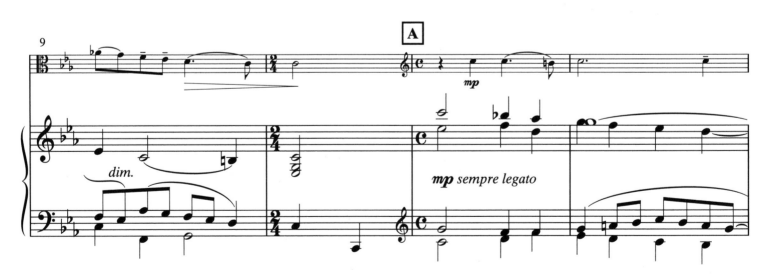

* Attributed to Thomas Tallis

6

Rondo

Jean Sibelius
1865-1957

Moderato assai ♩ = 72

G Meno mosso

* Original

* Original

Lovingly and reverently dedicated to the memory of Edvard Grieg

The Sussex Mummers' Christmas Carol

(By kind permission of Miss Lucy E. Broadwood)
Collected at Lyne, Sussex (England), by Miss Lucy E. broadwood

For my friend Herman Sandby,
in happy memory of joys in 1905

Percy Aldridge Grainger
1882-1961
Transcribed by Barbara Barber

Slowish, but flowing ♩ = 48

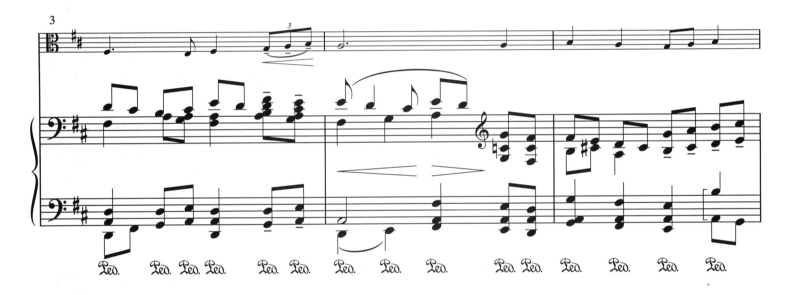

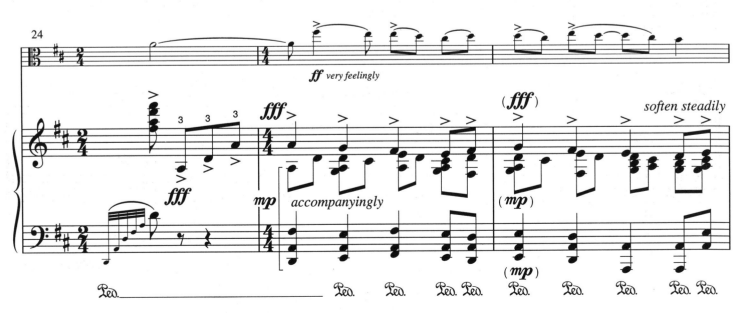

Nocturnes for Viola and Piano
Op. 186, No. 1

Johann Wenzel Kalliwoda
1801-1866

Op. 186 No. 2

Allegretto, ma un poco vivo ♩. = 80

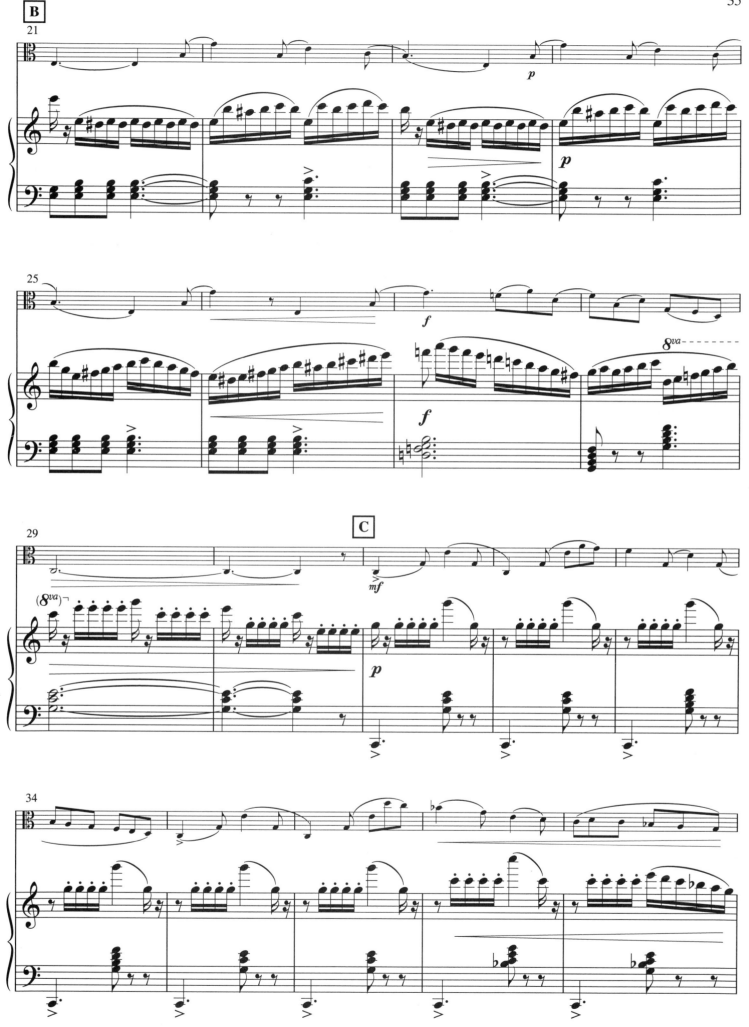

36

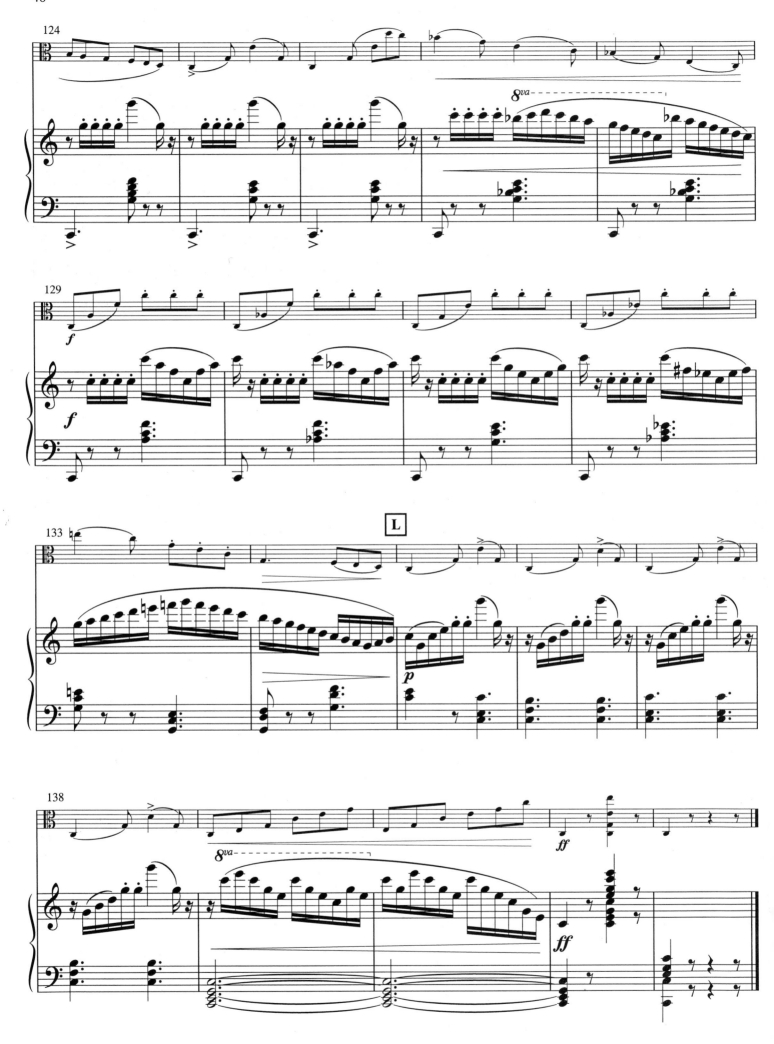

Op. 186, No. 6

Allegro moderato ♩ = 108

* Original

42

** Original

43

† Original

†† Original

Concerto in C Major
3rd Movement

Ivan Chandoshkin
1747-1804

Rondo "La Chasse"

Allegretto ♩ = 100

* F# in original.